Country Chic

COUNTRY CHIC

A Fresh Look at Contemporary Country Decor

LIEZEL NORVAL-KRUGER

PHOTOGRAPHY BY
CRAIG FRASER

FRIEDMAN/FAIRFAX
PUBLISHERS

First published in the United States
and Canada by

Friedman/Fairfax Publishers

15 West 26 Street

New York, NY 10010

Telephone (212) 685-6610

Fax (212) 685-1307

Please visit our website: www.metrobooks.com

Library of Congress Cataloging-in-Publication
Data available upon request

ISBN 1-58663-062-8

For NK Publishing:
Copy Editor: Ellen Fitz-Patrick
Art Director and Stylist: Liezel Norval-Kruger
Assistant Stylist: Holger Schutt

Color separations by Hirt and Carter
Printed in Singapore by Tien Wah Press
10 9 8 7 6 5 4 3 2 1

Distributed by Sterling Publishing Company, Inc.
387 Park Avenue South
New York, NY 10016
Distributed in Canada by Sterling Publishing
Canadian Manda Group
One Atlantic Avenue, Suite 105
Toronto, Ontario, Canada M6K 3E7
Distributed in Australia by
Capricorn Link (Australia) Pty Ltd.
P.O. Box 6651
Baulkham Hills, Business Centre,
NSW 2153, Australia

C O N T E N T S

INTRODUCTION

As the new millennium takes shape, we are living in a time of rapid change, with runaway developments in technology and a massive communication overload. We are so over-stimulated, many of us have a strong urge to return to a simpler lifestyle in tune with the rhythm of nature. Our surroundings can control and change the way we feel. Spending time in the country inevitably makes us feel refreshed and energized, which is why so many of us long to surround ourselves with elements that reflect a simple, relaxed rural existence.

Traditionally, country style meant a display of worldly possessions – cosy cluttered rooms with an abundance of frilled and piped soft furnishings and bunches of dried herbs and flowers suspended from the ceiling. These days, we prefer a more streamlined look that's relaxing on the eye and easier to maintain. Clutter and fancy decorative finishes have given way to clean, understated interiors. What distinguishes this new approach to country style is an honest mix of simplicity and sophistication that results in a contempo-

The new approach to country style is an honest mix of simplicity and sophistication

rary yet classic interior. Decorating is all about putting together interiors that make you feel good. *Country Chic* is quite simply a visual celebration of the new attitude in country decor with practical tips and advice to help you achieve the look. It also proves that a tiny house and budget does not preclude serious decorating. With a little resourcefulness and by making the most of what you have, you can turn any room into a visual feast.

Country style decorating is inspired by a melting pot of ideas and cultural influences from around the globe. The most well-known country interiors must surely be those of English country cottages with their laid-back comfort and romantic charm. The distinctive styles of Tuscan and Provençal farmhouses reflect the warm tones of the earth and a rustic aesthetic. Mediterranean country style draws inspiration from open landscapes bathed in brilliant sunlight and the deep blues of the ocean. The interiors have an inherent simplicity with clean lines, stark contrasts and basic furniture. The cool elegance

of traditional Swedish country style and the honest simplicity of American Shaker interiors have an understated sophistication that are consistent with the updated interpretation of country style. Different influences have led to many variations and interpretations of country style ranging from soft romantic florals to rustic simplicity. The fundamental values that underpin the different styles, however, remain the same.

In *Country Chic* I have picked out eight of the main looks in modern country decor: Rustic, Romantic, Fresh Floral, Modern Rose, Monotone, Natural, Nautical and Creative Color. For each of these styles I have attempted to show you an interpretation of the most important living areas of the house—the living room, dining room, kitchen, bedroom and bathroom. The luxury of having a different space allocated for each function in the home is definitely something of the past. In the modern home, where space tends to be limited, your kitchen often functions as a dining room, leads off your living area, and acts as a playroom. These areas are now designed to act as practical work areas with space for reading, doing your finances, or maybe even incorporating a home office. Your bedroom should be the ultimate refuge—a place of serenity where you can cast off the stresses of everyday life. Pretty bed linens and soothing colors create a truly restful and relaxing environment. In an increasingly frenetic world, bathrooms have grown in importance as havens for quiet reflection. Bathing is no longer simply a cleansing routine, it is a way of reviving energy and relieving daily stress.

You may not live a simple life, but walking into a home decorated in an updated country style will make you feel as though you do. The updated country style can be created with a multitude of different fabrics and furnishings, so feel free to experiment with a variety of materials to find the look that pleases you. The goal of this book is to inspire you to develop your own intepretation of Country Chic.

Today's country style is not about creating a fussy, chintzy **country** cottage, but more about inviting **nature** into your home with honest materials and a **simplicity** of design. You cannot always put a price

tag on beauty. Driftwood found on the **beach** or the color of wheat fields reflected in a

decorating scheme probably have more lasting value than the latest fashion innovation. Contemporary country furnishings are

UPDATED LOOK

welcoming and comfortable. Comfort is more about the **feel** of a fabric than the way it is styled. The emphasis is also not on slavishly trying to match up every item in the room, but all about casually **mixing** different shapes

and textures in an **honest**, natural way. Make the most of what you have by

finding new uses for existing pieces of furniture and don't be afraid to **update** the look. Get rid of the clutter and make room to live **life** to the fullest.

Nature

The longing for a country lifestyle is all about the need to slow the pace of life and get in touch with our natural instincts. Houses inspired by nature are those in which you can relax. Take inspiration from the beautiful shades of green in an undulating landscape, the sun-bleached whiteness of sea sand contrasting with the velvet blues in the swells of the ocean and the faded yellows of ripened wheat blowing in the wind. The colors, textures, and patterns of nature have the pulse of life and an intrinsic honesty, reminding us of a time when man still lived close to the earth. Wood, stone, and sand are more satisfying to our senses than synthetics, and contribute to a greater sense of well-being. Modern country furnishings are made from natural materials and have a simplicity of line and a sturdy, practical grace. Pure cotton bed linens, cashmere throws, knitted pillow covers, distressed wooden furniture, hardwearing canvas, and smooth pebbles picked up on the seashore all add a richness of texture and create a harmonious environment.

Simplicity

Modern country decorating is about creating a serene, relaxed environment with quiet lines where form and function are equally important. Furniture and accessories reflect the simplified, streamlined philosophy. Elaborate curtain treatments have been replaced with flowing reams of fabric hanging simply from curtain poles on rings or tab headers. Pattern, like floral print designs and checks and stripes, is used with restraint, and mostly as an accent. Lightly textured wallpapers are almost plain, in pale and earthy colors. Pillows are trimmed with buttons, natural fringing or tie details, and sofas and chairs have simple loose covers. Wooden furniture has a solid, rustic appearance, a plain design, and distressed painted surfaces to add texture and interest. Accessories should be used selectively and kept to a minimum.

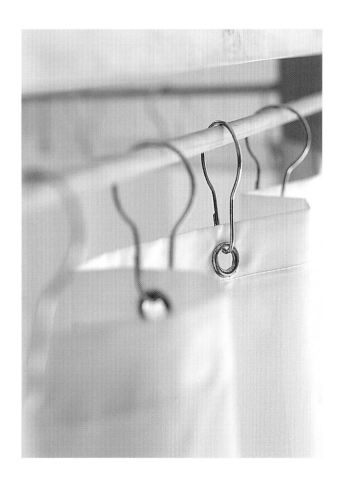

Lifestyle

The new look in country style decorating takes inspiration from the essence of rustic living—it is not merely a decorating style but a set of values, a way of life. Family values, friendship, caring, comfort, and repose are all part of this quality lifestyle. The modern approach is to create a home where the mind, body, and spirit reconnect. Our sense of touch is acute and is directly linked to our feelings. The taste and color of food enjoyed in the company of good friends stimulates our senses and creates an exuberant attitude to life. Earthy shapes and textures bring the simple and uncluttered lines of nature into your home, while natural light brings out the true shape and character of a room, and is as important as the decorations within.

Allow the past to live by creating an atmosphere of unspoiled rustic comfort. Take a break from the artificial pleasures of town and get in touch with intrinsic values and an  honest existence lived close to nature. Blend just a few old and new objects for an interesting mix and an understated aesthetic. Layer tweedy woven checks and hardwearing cotton canvases in warm earthy tones. With an eclectic collection of furniture that bears the mark of time, you can create a home with character and a thrown-together, mellow charm.

RUSTIC

Living Room

Comfort and cosiness define this rustic style, but the look relies on an unerring eye and disciplined order to give it a contemporary edge. Bulky sofas and easy chairs dressed in layers of earthy woven checks give an inviting sense of informality. Keep the colors subdued in dirty whites, grayish blues and greens, and muted terracottas. Distressed wooden furniture and textured wall finishes are absolutely crucial to the look. Distempered walls in warm tones create an appealing backdrop for wood and terracotta. Use accessories like generous-bellied jugs that double up as vases for loosely arranged bouquets.

clockwise from top left *Go to markets and auctions to hunt down stylish wooden furniture that's worn and comfortable. Time-worn texture adds character and a spirit of the past to provide a context for contemporary touches such as jute- and button-trim scatter pillows and simple curtain treatments.*

21

Kitchen

Rustic country kitchens are warm and friendly and the real heart of the home where dogs, children, and visitors congregate. The all-in-one sociable kitchen with a spacious eating area has replaced the formal dining room. Mixing the functional with the decorative, it is the perfect space for work and play. Crisp formality and symmetry are shunned in favour of casual comfort. Dinner plates, table linens, and cutlery are housed and displayed in an antique dresser placed conveniently close to the table. Visit junk and antique shops often to build up a good selection of antique crockery and cutlery, or raid your mother or grandmother's cupboards for any unwanted pieces. The beauty of old china is that it mixes and matches effortlessly. Although cupboards and armoires are the perfect answer to hide any clutter, open

left *Decorate empty wall space cleverly and usefully with an antique coat rack. Sunhats, jackets, and walking shoes or boots are easily accessible for an impromptu ramble.*

clockwise from top left *Cupboards and open shelving built in alcoves in the wall provide useful storage for kitchenware. Grow herbs in pots to have easy access to fresh flavors. For the best salads, make dressings with extra virgin olive oil, freshly squeezed lemon juice, chopped herbs, and garlic. Invest in a simple metal chandelier for cosy candle-lit dinners. Cloth-covered books add a nostalgic touch.*

shelves can be practical and decorative. Arrange displays of condiments, screw-top glass containers, crockery, and other kitchen equipment. Grow herbs in terracotta pots on windowsills and use them as aromatic table decorations. They are also incredibly handy to have at arm's length when cooking. Stick to rustic wooden furniture that has stood the test of time. Don't worry about matching styles perfectly, as different shapes and colors of old oak and pine can live together quite comfortably. Use woven check fabrics to make informal loose covers for chairs or tablecloths or to line the backs of old dressers.

Bedroom

Textures are central to the attractively simple character of this rustic country bedroom: terracotta wallpaper, sisal carpeting, a plain cotton rug, sturdy furniture, and simply hung woven check curtains. An exquisitely crafted patchwork quilt gives the bedroom traditional but unfussy charm. Despite—or rather because of—the eclecticism, this room has a particular harmony and synergy. Creating this look in a city dwelling has become easy now that the essential accoutrements of country style are easily

available from decorating boutiques and chain stores alike. For an authentic effect, search for distressed pieces of furniture at flea markets and antique shops. Choose your furniture with a multi-purpose in mind: a wooden chair can function just as well as a bedside table; a blanket chest provides storage and also doubles as extra seating or as a coffee table in front of a sofa.

clockwise from top left

Combine pure cotton bed linens in plain creams with warm woven checks in earthy tones. The fussy look of old-fashioned quilts is updated with subtler, simpler designs.

Put attractive pieces of left-over fabric to good use by tying documents together or to replace ribbons when gift-wrapping.

Well-worn furniture has lots of character and combines well with earthy, woven checks.

Bathroom

This bathroom is given instant character and style with a free-standing basin featuring strong masculine lines and contemporary, elongated taps inspired by a traditional Victorian design. A small mirror with a dark wooden frame simply hung with a jute cord adds contrast and a sense of nostalgia. The bathroom is spare and orderly, with fittings and accessories carefully selected for their simplicity and intrinsically pure design. Washing should always be a sensual pleasure, so indulge in refined soaps with warm, spicy fragrances such as sandalwood. Add a luxurious touch with embroidered pure cotton hand towels.

right *The warm scent of sandalwood enhances an atmosphere that is spare yet sensual.*

31

from left *Surround yourself with warm, spicy colors for an interior that radiates earthy comfort and style.*

No country kitchen is complete without the aroma of freshly baked breads or pies. Collect old silverware to mix with antique china. Keep them shiny by wrapping individual pieces of cutlery in tinfoil when not in use.

Look for accessories with style and char-acter, such as distressed picture frames. Make pillows with simple tie details: cut and sew a plain pillow cover of 18 inches by 18 inches (45cm by 45cm) with an inner flap like a pillowcase. Make four ties with a finished width of 1 inch (2.5cm) and a length of at least 6 inches (15cm). Pin the ties a ¹/₂ inch (1cm) inside the opening, spacing them equally, and machine stitch several times for strength.

e l e m e n t s

Heighten the senses with the calmness and simplicity of natural, neutral colors and textures. Blur the boundaries between inside and outside by embracing the tones of wood, stone, and earth.

Explore the richness, variety, and intrinsic beauty of naturally occurring materials. Surrender to whites, creams, gray-browns, and taupes to reflect light and create an atmosphere of space. Roughly painted wood, heavy woven cotton fabrics, delicate muslin, and furnishings at once practical and elegant create a restful style in tune with the rhythm of nature.

NATURALS

Living Room

The neutral tones of white, cream and taupe create a graceful, restful living room. Contemporary touches include simple, painted wooden furniture, plain loose covers for chairs and sofas as well as pure white vases and bowls with clean, fluid lines. Complement the look with understated window treatments such as this soft-structured blind. If you prefer curtains, choose simple tab, or tie-tab designs and hang them from a wooden or wrought-iron rod. Ties, tabs, or other imaginative headings are a feature in themselves and work best with plain fabrics. Be careful to steer away from elaborate finial designs. Anything too ornate will jar the atmosphere of natural simplicity. A basic neutral color scheme is versatile and well-suited to modern living. Its flexibility offers potential for introducing other colors with the use of flowers or decorating

right *Contrast the homey feel of rough, worn wooden surfaces with clean-cut shapes and smooth textures for a thoroughly modern feel.*

accessories. Try introducing black in the form of script-design fabrics for a graphic, modern feel or add scatter pillows and throws in spicy brick and mustard for a more earthy result. With a natural interior there are a variety of choices when it comes to flooring. Explore different materials, from quarry tiles and limed oak to sisal and slate. Wood provide warmth and refinement, while slate and terracotta add roughness and texture. Walls should ideally be painted in matte white or given surface interest and warmth with textured wallpapers or ragged paint finishes in natural or earthy tones.

clockwise from top left *Modern yet comfortable settings need large-scale sofas in simple styles. Invest in accessories with clean lines such as these understated limestone bowls.*
Collect bits and pieces from nature and make displays in bowls or picture frames.
Loosely tie cotton rope around basic white candles to make simple displays.
For interest, opt for brown textured and striped wallpapers.

Dining Room

This dining room reflects a spartan simplicity reminiscent of medieval monasteries. The windows are left unadorned, allowing light to flood through. Keeping them free of curtains or blinds gives an added feeling of spaciousness and the changing light adds to the atmospheric effect. The only luxurious touch is the cream cotton tablecloth that falls all the way to the floor. For a more rustic look, paint the cotton with an oil-based interior paint, then machine-wash, to crackle the paint and let it form a textured,

mottled effect. Hunt for under-stated utilitarian tableware with pleasing shapes. Some of the best designs of plain white or cream china can be found inexpensively at departmental stores or even certain supermarkets. Add to the atmosphere by mixing white china with plain glassware like glass hur-ricane lamps or votives placed in small tumblers.

left *In a dining room that raises simplicity to an art form, the flavors of the food that is served can be fully appreciated. Savor a simple meal of home-made linguine, perhaps with a pesto made from basil grown in your own garden.*

Kitchen

Natural and painted wood, stainless steel, and plain cream cotton fabric are combined in a kitchen that is both rustic and modern. The clutter is contained within a tall cabinet with chicken wire mesh doors lined with cream curtains to create a layering of tones. Make use of a hanging wall system and butcher's hooks for a practical and aesthetic way of organizing cooking utensils and tea towels. If you are unable to source a ready-made version, try assembling something similar from whatever is available at your local hardware store.

clockwise from top left *Simple everyday glass tumblers have an instrinsic beauty of their own and look particularly good when grouped en masse.*
The well-worn surface of this old table was left untouched to preserve its pleasingly weathered texture, but the base and legs were painted white for a clean, crisp look.
The aroma and texture of food is as much a part of the charac-ter of a kitchen as the decor.

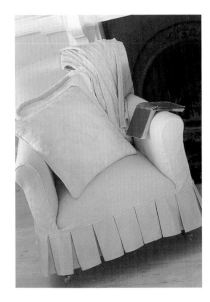

clockwise from top left *Give softness to spartan simplicity with a simple muslin drape.*
Choose jacquard bedspreads for their luxurious texture.
Add atmosphere with candle holders arranged in neat rows.
Mix natural finishes such as distressed wood and jute trim with the clean lines of wrought iron.
Make reading enjoyable with comfortable seating.
White and cream combine perfectly in a natural scheme.

Bedroom

To create an intimate atmosphere with softness and comfort, a simple wrought iron four-poster bed (previous page) is teamed with soft, sheer muslin curtains, allowing diffused light to illuminate the room. The bed is simply dressed with a plain cotton canopy with broad ties, and accessorized with bulky bolsters so that it forms the focus of attention in this spacious room. The inside of the canopy is trimmed with narrow ties to secure the canopy to the bedframe. Natural equals pure—a theme carried through in this bedroom with a minimum of decoration. Everything is kept simple, from the bedcovers to the dado rail. Be sure to invest in good quality, pure cotton white bed linens and soft wool blankets in shades of cream to add a luxurious touch. There are all sorts of beds that suit the natural look. Whitewashed wood, wrought iron, or a plain daybed suitable for both sitting and sleeping are just some of the options. If you have an existing bed that does not quite fit with the look, consider dressing it with a plain cream loose cover. Add detail with a pleated skirt and tortoiseshell buttons.

Bathroom

Create your own soul-soothing haven with a bathroom that radiates freshness and simplicity. The spare lines of this bathroom bring an air of serenity to a quick dip or longer linger in a roomy slipper bath. Subdued neutrals, simple window treatments and understated furniture allow light to become an important element. A bathroom cabinet with glass doors is ideal for storing and displaying crisp white towels, toothbrushes and delectable toiletries.

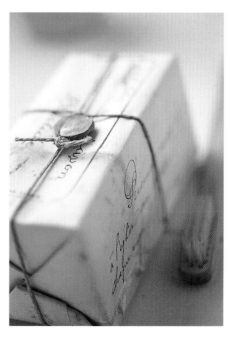

from left *Nature is filled with color but the true natural palette includes an understated range of creams, gray-browns, and taupes.*

Collect pebbles and interesting seeds from nature and display them in wooden or limestone bowls.

Ordinary wooden clothes pegs make a fun alternative to the usual curtain holders. Clip plain lengths of sheer fabric to natural rope or thin wooden rods for beautifully understated curtain treatments.

Make the most of the magnificent colors and shapes of autumn leaves by display- ing them in frames. Crumple up ordinary white or cream paper for a textured back- ing and cut to the required size. Stick your chosen leaf on the brown paper using double-sided tape or glue and place in a wooden or distressed finish frame. Keep detailing simple with plain button, natural cord and simple tie trims.

e l e m e n t s

There is something about soft, sun-mellowed English garden roses in pale pastels that is both nostalgic and marvelously romantic. Give a breezy, open feel to your surroundings, and make your home a restful

place. Imagine being in a country garden. Surrender to soft creamy pastel roses rambling up tea and cream backgrounds—a design classic that never fades. Give florals a contemporary feel by combining them with simple shapes, clean colors and understated accessories for a look that is fresh, charming and serene.

ROMANTIC

Living Room

Traditional English rose designs are given a new lease on life and a thoroughly contemporary edge when teamed with a simple, neutral palette of white and cream. Clean, understated lines play up romantic curves and soft floral fabric designs. The emphasis is on natural textures, with selective floral accents in the blinds and accessories. Make the most of limited space with unusual, creative room layouts. In this instance (previous page) the sitting and dining areas have been combined. The elegant white-painted dinner table forms the focal point of the room with living spaces created around it. The footstool provides extra seating space at the table and doubles as a coffee table in front of the sofa. When the dining room table is not in use, it acts as an area for displaying books and china, or as a convenient working surface. The overall effect is modern and tranquil.

Kitchen

In the kitchen an old wooden table is used in combination with a selection of mismatched chairs (junk-shop finds) to create a cozy feeling. It is child-friendly, comfortable, and welcoming. Antique pine is great because it is already worn; a few crayon marks won't ruin a table. The look is given a soft romantic edge with simple floral cushions, a scalloped roman blind and an eclectic mix of kitchenware.

clockwise from top *Collect fine china with floral designs from antique shops or rescue unwanted pieces from relatives. Store the dishes in open shelves or cupboards to show off their charms but do not treat them only as showpieces. Turn every day into a special occasion by using favorite cups and plates daily.*
Floral tablecloths give an instant lift to the breakfast table. Buy lengths of fabric from end of rolls or discontinued lines and hem them for inexpensive and quick table linens.
An old enamel colander makes an effective fruit bowl.

Fine porcelain cups with sweet floral designs are thrown together with distressed metal canisters and old enamel teapots. If you like, dress the chairs with tied slip covers or floppy pancake seat cushions. Be sure, however, to use fully washable cotton, as kitchens require a lot of cleaning – especially if there are children around. To keep the look light, mix painted and whitewashed wooden details (such as the baby high chair and food cabinet) with darker wood. Promote unused chests of drawers and dressers from the bedroom to the kitchen to create freestanding storage space. Give them a face-lift with a coat of paint or special effect. Stick to white walls to provide a clean backdrop for more fussy, nostalgic touches like the window architrave hung with baskets, dried flowers, and strings of garlic. White-painted walls are effective in making a small room look big, and a dingy room bright.

left *Decant cereals, rice, coffee, and other dry foods into metal and glass canisters for an attractive storage solution.*

Bedroom

Tones of cream and pink can create a clear and calm mood that need not be frumpy—just steer clear of frills and keep it understated. Confine your scheme to a backdrop of white or cream and accessorize with floral touches. A modern, romantic, and ultra-feminine retreat is created with a white antique cast iron bed, a luxurious ecru jacquard bedspread, and a gauzy sheer muslin blind that is simply rolled and tied up. For a more structured look, consider roman blinds with

clockwise from top left *Add a romantic touch to ordinary flip-flops with artificial rose posies. Open shelves provide unusual, practical, and decorative storage for clothing and personal items. Give romantic florals a new look by using them sparingly against a backdrop of white and cream. Dressing tables are given character with informal displays of favorite items.*

A small bench makes an informal and effective side-table.

plain or scalloped edges. The walls and all the furniture are painted white. White paint not only provides a serene background, it also unifies an assortment of flea-market furniture. Make sure that old paint or varnish is stripped off properly with sandpaper or stripping solution before applying a fresh coat of paint. A small wooden bench acts as a side table with black and white postcards simply nailed to the wall above it. Architectural detail is added with a white wooden dresser that is used for storing clothing and linens. Give it a personal touch with favorite collectibles and family photographs.

Bathroom

Light a candle, have a glass of wine handy, put on your favorite music, and indulge in natural, fragrant pleasure by throwing freshly picked lavender or rosemary sprigs into a steaming hot bath of water. Then sink back and relax with a good book. A steel bath rack with book-stand is the perfect answer for keeping reading matter dry and storing soaps and bath oils in antique bottles. Look for an old Victorian tub and combine it with wooden floors and white-washed wooden furniture.

THE RAINS CAME

energy which had always animated all his great bulk and turned
mere weight into strength was gone, and he appeared dull, inert and
heavy, the hard line vanished from his jaw, the muscles of his big
face all flaccid. He had suddenly become simply a repulsive mass
of flesh.

And then she remembered a little vaguely what had happened the
night before in the palace and the quarrel that had taken place in
her bedroom, and she was filled suddenly with shame and a loathing
for herself, not because of Ransome or even because she was pro-
miscuous—she felt no shame for any of the adventures she had had
outside marriage—but because she had lived for nearly ten years
with this gross mass of flesh which lay in the bed of teakwood and
mother-of-pearl, that she had yielded herself again and again to him
with indifference. All the other men—all of them—had at least
been beautiful in one way or another, and she thought at once of
Ransome and how different his body was, how slim and hard in spite
of all his drinking and dissipation. Looking down at Heston she
thought, "Whether he lives or dies I'll never sleep with him again."
But she wished shamelessly that he would die, for she knew that as
long as she lived she would always see him thus, betrayed by his
illness, heavy, gross, purple-faced, with his mouth hanging open a
little; and each time that she saw him she would remember that she
had prostituted her fine slim body to him again and again. Only
with him, her husband, had she ever been a prostitute. With all
the others there had been pleasure and even sometimes love. Heston
alone had ever paid her.

Leaning over the bed, she knew that Bates was watching her,
dankly curious to see how she would behave, and she knew that
she must put on some sort of show which, although it would probably
not deceive Bates, would make him believe in her good intentions.
She was aware that in his servant's way he already knew too much
about her.

She said, as if she were a devoted wife, "Albert! Albert! It's
Edwina." The dull pale blue eyes opened a little way but they only
looked into space, far beyond her, without focusing. He made a
faint grunting sound and then the eyes closed again. A second time she
tried with no more result, and then she said, "I'll write a note,
Bates. We'd better send it off at once. I'll bring it to you. You'd
better stay here to watch."

In her own room she took out her writing-case and a bottle of

from left *Pink and green, exquisitely matched in nature, are the perfect colors for romantic and restful interiors. Give traditional floral designs a new lease on life by choosing simple, un-fussy window treatments. Distressed wood and white painted wicker emphasizes the feeling of lightness. Search around at markets and second-hand stores for old faded flower prints. For a relaxed look, prop them up on tables and dressers, or if you want a more formal look, group them on the wall. Ensure that your house is always filled with masses of voluptuous roses by planting rose bushes or climbing varieties in the garden or in terracotta pots. Collect delicate antique china with floral designs for just the right mood.*

e l e m e n t s

Clean, sleek lines, open spaces, and the impact of strong color combine to create an environment radiating relaxed modern sophistication. Get hooked on graphic patterns and architectural shapes mixed with natural touches like sisal carpets, chairs with rush seats, and woven cotton fabrics. Use furniture sparingly. Woven stripes, subtle checks against a plain backdrop, and minimal accessories create a grand yet restrained impression.

MONOTONE

Living Room

The sophisticated look of this living area, which incorporates both sitting and dining, is linear and spare. The sense of space is maximized by keeping the color scheme and furnishings very understated. The almost abstract quality of the room is emphasised by the strong lines of the bold striped tablecloth, and furniture is minimal for dramatic impact. Though furniture is sparse, it is an interesting mix of different styles: country style ladder-back chairs with rush seats, classic slipcovered upholstery, and an elegant white painted console table. Typical of a modern, pared down approach, furni-

clockwise from top *The white paint finish of the console table accentuates its fluid, elegant lines. Choose muslin curtains to maximize the light. Muslin brings a softness to contemporary curtain treatments. Chairs with rush seats add texture and a natural touch to the scheme. Use generously proportioned chairs with convenient slipcovers to accentuate the scale of the room.*

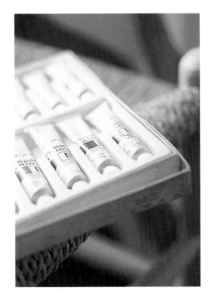

ture has multiple functions: here, the dining table is used for eating, working, and reading. Sheer curtains allow filtered light to illuminate the space. A muslin curtain looks best when it has sufficient fullness to show off its soft, easy-drape characteristics, but that does not mean that you have to resort to frilly finishes. Try tab-header curtains with inverted pleats positioned to correlate with each tab, or make curtains with a heading tape of your choice and attach to curtain rings by means of knotted ribbons. Keep accessories to the bare minimum and stick to black and white prints and etchings in black wooden or aluminum frames.

Kitchen

Balance functionality with aesthetics in a kitchen that is a perfect blend of modern and country. Simple stripes and checks contrast with warmer touches like the collection of kitchenware displayed on open shelving. This kind of shelving is inexpensive yet effective and can easily be put together in an afternoon if you have the time and basic tools. Alternatively, hire a carpenter to build them to your specifications.

clockwise from top left

Smooth white ceramics lend a modern touch to the country kitchen.

The striped paint effect on the wall is boldly graphic but also charming and fun. The wider the stripe, the more up-to-date the look.

Overhead pendant lights in brushed aluminum provide a pool of light to subtly illuminate work surfaces.

Make the most of natural ingredients at hand by experimenting with different focaccia toppings. Chop mixed fresh herbs and sprinkle on the bread with crushed garlic and coarse sea salt, or cover with a layer of roasted vegetables and shavings of parmesan cheese.

Bedroom

A combination of clean-cut furniture and texturized color is used to create a look that is uncluttered but not stark. The mood is mellow with a soft two-tone mix that is easy on the eye. Brick and cream checks are warm, laid-back, and elegant. The design of the wrought iron bed is very simple, allowing you to dress it up or down with soft furnishings. Give an interesting twist to traditional four-poster curtains by hanging them from curtain rings instead of directly onto the bedframe. Let the curtains drape to the floor or tie them back simply and effectively with a hemmed length of contrasting fabric. Understated window treatments keep the focus on the simple yet sumptuous bed. Leave the windows bare or dress them with plain roman blinds.

opposite *Warmth without excess is the secret to the tranquil simplicity of this bedroom.*

Bathroom

A Victorian-style footed tub, gold-plated faucet and shower head, and lavishly draped shower curtains transform a functional bathroom into something more elegant and luxurious. The curtain is at once decorative and practical, lined with a layer of white plastic to protect it from splashes. Details like the delightful metal soap tray on the shower pipe give that added touch of luxury and make this room a haven after a long day at work.

clockwise from top left *The elegant shape of the roll-top bathtub with ball-and-claw feet forms an unusual contrast with rustic sisal carpeting.*
Bathing is certainly one of life's most rejuvenating pleasures. Enhance the experience with fragrant bath oils and salts.
Walls of Scandinavian blue add understated sophistication to the brick and cream color scheme.
Add a refined touch with white embroidered waffle-weave towels.
Japanese house shoes are a must to slip your feet into after a relaxing bath.

clockwise from left *Red, cream, and a soft shade of blue make a striking and sophisticated color scheme.*
Add bold stripes to a country kitchen. You'll need: Water-based white paint; red glaze; varnish. Step by step: 1. Measure the wall width and divide it by the number of repeats. 2. Apply two coats of white paint. 3. Mark stripe spacing along ceiling edge. Drop a plumb line from each mark and pencil in the stripe edges. 4. Mask off the edges of the stripes. Using a broad brush and red glaze, paint the stripes, wiping the painted area with a soft cloth before it dries to form a textured effect. 5. Apply a coat of varnish. Hanging buckets are an innovative storage alternative for vegetables and fruit. Add interest to a dining chair with a cushion attached with criss-cross ties. A checked border gives a plain cream runner a graphic effect.

e l e m e n t s

Celebrate the sensual pleasure of a generous burst of velvety deep red roses with their heavy, sweet scent and delicate texture. The dramatic

sophistication of shades of dark pink, red, green, and mustard are perfect for modern, bold rose print designs. Elegant woven jacquard fabrics, streamlined furniture, textured wallpapers, and quirky decorating accessories, mixed with touches of dark and distressed wood give a fresh look to things past and present. The look is a sensual and seductive interior.

MODERN ROSE

Living Room

Traditional rose-print designs take on a new identity with boldly painted large scale motifs in strong colors. These new floral prints are best displayed against a sober white backdrop or given added impact with textured wallpaper. The daring combination of robust rose-patterned curtains, clean-cut upholstered furniture, dark wood, and warm terracotta wallpaper epitomizes a relaxed contemporary mood. Be sure to steer away from too dark a hue on the walls as this will only subdue the impact and up-to-date effect. Accessorize with quirky touches such as small oblong cushions and the pure lines of shapely vases.

Dining Room

In this dining room, a bold floral curtain is set against the understated appeal of white tongue-and-groove walls and a white-washed timber floor. Combined with luxurious silver and crystal touches, the look is modern, sophisticated, and elegant. Simplicity of styling is key, with the gilded and crystal accessories sparkling against a backdrop of crisp white table linens. You don't have to spend a fortune on expensive fabric to create this look. Buy a few yards of white or cream cotton fabric and sew up a simple tablecloth. Add a broad border with mitered corners in the same fabric for a finished look. The extra weight of the border will make the tablecloth hang beautifully.

clockwise from top *Set the table with heavy silverware, mismatched antique fine china, and crystal glassware.*
An inner border of unpatterned fabric adds a linear touch to bold floral curtains.
Introduce a touch of luxury with rich woven jacquards.

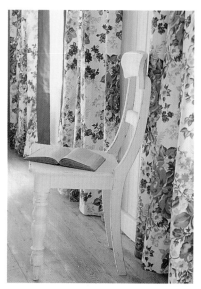

Kitchen

Combining utility and aesthetics, this kitchen has been designed with traditional touches, yet the end result is clean and modern. An all-white palette is given a bold splash of color with a simple floral tablecloth. Keep the look uncluttered with clever storage and minimal accessorizing. The cream painted console table with a convenient bottom shelf provides a simple form of open storage for pots and pans, while the tall cupboard with wire mesh doors makes a feature of blue-and-white dishware. The folding chairs are a clever space-saving alternative to fixed or heavy wooden furniture and can easily be stowed to create more space, or moved to other rooms when extra seating is needed.

clockwise from top left *Add color by making simple displays with fruit on white china plates.*
Cut a piece of pegboard and frame it in a modern steel picture frame for a handy and attractive display option for cooking utensils and pans.
Antique blue and white china gives a stylish edge to any decor scheme.
Ensure a clean and uncluttered look with plenty of drawers and cupboard space.

Bedroom

In this bedroom the essence of modern romanticism is captured through the combination of simple clean lines, touches of softness, and bursts of bold color against a white backdrop. Keep the look understated with contemporary floral-lined curtains—they allow a hint of romance without overpowering the room. Window treatments are often an afterthought, which is a pity, because the right window treatment can transform a room, emphasizing the effect of natural light and expressing a particular style. The curtains in this modest country bedroom have simple tab headers, but a fuller curtain with a ruffled edge and fabric ties fixing the curtain to a curtain pole would also work with this decor. Be thoughtful in your choice of curtain treatment.

right *Mix traditional frilled pillowcases with clean modern styles like those with Oxford borders or narrow tie details. Use contrasting fabrics to accentuate the design and provide texture. Small gingham checks work well with large-scale floral designs.*

Make sure that the selected style suits the particular fabric you have chosen and the dimensions of the window, and fits in with the style of the interior. Rich brocades made up in elegant pelmets and formal tie-backs will look out of place in a country-style interior. Luscious layers of bedding and simple frilled pillow-cases give a sense of comfort and sensuality. Contrast floral-print bedding with crisp white sheets and a white or cream comforter. Choose a wooden whitewashed bedstead to create a fresh, modern effect. Darker wooden elements can also be introduced into this scheme very successfully, but the end result will be a more traditional look.

clockwise from top left *A pre-dominantly pastel pink and blue palette of traditional rose print designs are traded in favor of more saturated hues of dark pink, red, green, and mustard. Use textured and trellis design wallpapers to add a backdrop of color.*

Look for contemporary accessories with a floral theme. White embroidered bed linens provide a simple base for layering with floral bedcovers.

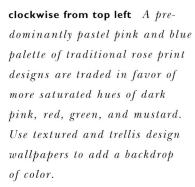

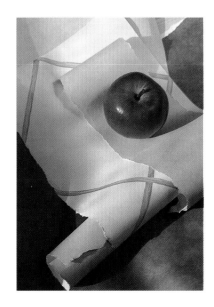

Bathroom

Pleasure meets purpose in this bathroom with a generous view through the window, allowing contemplation of the garden while you are soaking in the bath. The free-standing bath is shielded on either side by two shower curtains suspended from simple wooden screens. A shower is an invigorating wake-up call in the morning and excellent therapy against the stresses of the day at night. Invest in a good shower system—the best have powerful delivery and a big showerhead to evenly distribute the water. Bathroom floors need to be splashproof—you can waterproof a wooden floor by sealing the joints and coating the entire floor with boat varnish.

clockwise from top left *This faucet set combines modern plumbing with old-fashioned style.*
Fragrant soaps and loofahs are great for a gentle exfoliation with a creamy lather.
Rack-style soap dishes allow water to drain off soaps so they last longer.
Shower screens offer an attractive free-standing alternative to traditional shower curtain arrangments.

from left *Green balances red and dark pink accents to create a boldly elegant interior.*

Distressed wooden frames do double duty as room dividers and shower screens. Use metal hooks or fabric ties to fix the shower curtain to the screen. Leave walls white or add color with wallpapers in saturated tones. Borders give a neat finish and decorative interest to pillowcases. The correct method to make an Oxford flap is to attach a separate border with mitered corners. However, there is a quicker way if you are not using a contrasting fabric: 1. Make a simple square pillow cover allowing extra width for the required depth of the border. 2. Measure in from the edge the required depth of the border, draw a square, and sew along this line. Play with quirky accents such as small oblong cushions.

e l e m e n t s

Take inspiration from the sea: create an atmosphere of true relaxation all year round. Explore the creative potential of tactile elements; dazzling color and weatherbeaten texture  inspired by the seashore. Revel in the blues of the ocean and sunbleached whites teamed with beachcombing spoils to capture the style of simple seaside living. Hardwearing canvas fabrics, generously proportioned furniture, white tongue-and-groove walls, yacht-inspired decorating accessories and rope details create a look that is unaffected and truly refreshing.

N A U T I C A L

clockwise from top left *Fabric colors can change a room as much as the impact of paint. For a backdrop of color use brick, terracotta, or large trellis wall-papers. Don't worry about matching pillow covers with the rest of the furnishings; it is much more interesting to try out contrasting fabric shades.*

Accessories made of natural materials add texture and bring life to your surroundings.

Living Room

A casual, relaxed atmosphere is created by mixing comfortable slip-covered sofas with wicker and distressed wooden furniture. Both stylish and functional, the blue upholstery is the perfect background for understated, contemporary pillows with button and rope details. The book shelves with layered white paint finish, offer an ideal way to integrate storage with the overall style of the room. The predominantly blue and white theme is warmed up with splashes of mustard. Nautical artifacts are spread across the white painted mantel and coffee table. The way you display favorite things is all part of creating order and giving your living space a personalized look. Use natural elements to create simple displays: try stacking pebbles from the beach or filling shadow boxes with shells and other bits and pieces from the shoreline.

Dining Room

The simple, but striking look of this dining room hinges on the play of textures. Natural tones of ecru and mustard are contrasted with black metal, unfinished wood, and distressed finishes. An understated nautical touch is created with stylish slip-covered chairs featuring rope detailing, simple metal hurricane lanterns, and bundles of rope informally tied to a chunky metal rod with seagrass twine. Look for old maps at the library or municipal archives for interesting but cost effective wall hangings.

Kitchen

A comfortable, cheerful kitchen with a utilitarian feel is created with a mix of old and new. The convenience of the present is combined with a nostalgic love of the past. Create a quirky charm with chairs of various shapes and contemporary touches of stainless steel and galvanized metal for contrast. Collectibles and personal mementos help to create an atmosphere of individuality. Seek out old knives

clockwise from top left

Contrast the clean look of woven stripes with the warm feel of antique furniture. Eating is one of life's sensual pleasures. Simply stuff salmon trout with parsley, garlic, and butter, and place on the grill.
Bags with tie openings are practical, look good, and are incredibly easy to make using your sewing machine at home. Collect shells from the beach and glue or sew them onto bags. Wire mesh cupboards are a practical and decorative way to display china or groceries. For a homespun feel with an updated edge, use galvanized metal buckets to hold fruit or grow herbs.

with bone handles at antique shops specializing in cutlery and silverware, and collect basic white plates and simple glass tumblers. Simple displays of old kitchen utensils suggest a confident cook and the possibility of appetizing meals to be eaten at leisure. Storage solutions are the key to creating a well-organized kitchen. An old storage cupboard can be given a facelift by the addition of new doors, in this case wire mesh ones. Larger pieces are incredibly useful for housing plates, glasses, herbs, and just about any other kitchen paraphernalia. If you have an unfitted kitchen, combine a minimum of built-in elements (a sink, stove, and worktop) with simple freestanding cabinets and tables. The great advantage of an unfitted kitchen is, of course, the fact that the cabinets and cupboards can be taken with you if you move.

opposite *Collect shells, pebbles, and other bits and pieces from the beach to devise interesting diplays on windowsills and small tables.*

Bedroom

Different tones of blue, from chambray to steel, lend a seaside air to this bedroom. The airy feeling is enhanced with fresh, bright walls: apply matte white paint to the lower half of the wall and a sandy wash to the upper portion above the dado. A space saving tub chair is ideal for reading and relaxing. If you prefer a more natural look, introduce a wicker chair—it mixes well with a nautical theme and is a good alternative to an upholstered chair. A small white-washed table replaces the usual bedside table, creating a more casual effect and providing a place to display decorative boats, pebbles, or toiletries.

left *Whimsical objects add a jaunty touch to the coastal theme. A personal touch comes from a selection of photos in blue and white leather-trimmed frames.*

Bathroom

This spacious bathroom features the delicious textures of fluffy white towels, natural loofah, and smooth pebbles picked up from the seashore. Inset shelves next to the fireplace are covered with a roman blind—made with panels of canvas in contrasting tones to create a flag-like effect. The walls and furniture are in tones of white to provide a clean backdrop for strong accents of navy blue, mustard, and brick. To enhance the look, buy toiletries in blue and white packaging, see-through glycerine soaps, and accessories in natural stone.

clockwise from top *Display bath oils and body lotions in blue bottles on open shelves, or keep within reach on a steel or chrome-plated rack. Attach hooks in a row on the wall to create hanging space for sumptuous bathrobes, towels, or clothing.*
Tones of blue, white, and sand create a serene effect in this nautical bathroom.

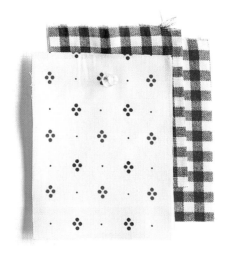

from left *Blue, the color of sea and sky, is the dominant shade in a nautical decor. Blue is peaceful and refreshing, generating a sense of well-being.*

Choose sofas and chairs with clean, understated lines and cover with plain, striped, or checked canvas. Complement the look with black-and-white photographs or prints in whitewashed frames, or simply nail them to the wall.

Rope and eyelet detail give a distinctly nautical feel to chairs, footstools, curtains, and blinds.

Look for typical nautical accessories such as boats and lighthouses. Accessorize with blue striped and checkered pillows. Add atmosphere to the bedroom, bathroom, or dining room with basic hurricane lanterns. They also look great dotted around the garden on a sultry summer evening.

e l e m e n t s

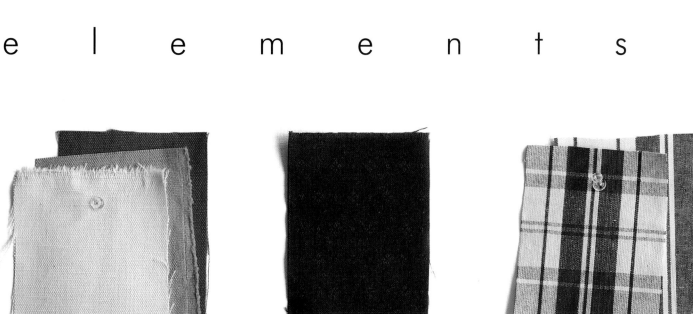

Bring to life the sultry and heady fragrance of a long, late summer afternoon with colors that are refreshing and modern. Indulge in abundant bursts of flowers and the distinctive scents and flavors of seasonal crops flourishing in the garden. Let a warm sum-

mer breeze blow through your rooms decorated in sunny yellows, restful greens, and lavender blues. Slip loose covers onto your chairs, dress up windows with understated floral curtains, and throw in a touch of wicker, metal, painted wood, and gold for smart summer living.

F R E S H   F L O R A L

Living Room

The atmosphere of a room is determined by the color scheme. Rich yellow, green, and blue floral designs mixed with canvas fabrics in blue and cream create a fresh, sunny feeling. Although traditional floral patterns are an important element of this look, the total picture is by no means fussy, sweet, or cloying. The secret lies in keeping it simple: pure shapes, streamlined furniture, natural elements, and understated styling. In this livng room the yellow textured wallpaper brightens up the look, while wicker and whitewashed wood add a contemporary touch. Deciding on whether to wallpaper or paint your walls can be a tough decision. Paint is easier as most people can do it themselves. You can also get a beautiful result quickly and touch up any mistakes. When choosing your color you must remember, however, that your result will be influenced by both the wall's underlying color and reflected light. If you are after more than just a plain color, wallpaper is definitely the answer—unless, of course, you are particularly talented with a brush and have

clockwise from top left *Woven throws in slightly faded greens and yellows are handy to drape over a sofa or chair.*

Stick to plain accessories with subtle details to create an unfussy look. Wicker furniture is eco friendly and works well indoors and outdoors. Cushions provide a layering of pattern. Choose simple designs with contemporary trims such as natural or jute cording and button and tie details.

clockwise from top left *There is nothing like the combination of wicker and the color green to evoke images of a summer garden. Combine with trellis wallpaper and tapestry cushions for a colonial touch.*
Look for interesting handpainted pots and fill with plants.
Botanical accesories in metal add an eclectic feel.
Handpainted shadow pictures with topiary designs work well against textured wallpapers.

plenty of time and patience. With wallpaper you can get anything from textured finishes to stripes, geometric patterns, trellis designs, and stenciled effects. Among the advantages of wallpaper are that you can form an immediate impression of how it will look before you hang it, and it will cover up most imperfections on the wall. When deciding on a particular wall treatment, you must remember that it will influence the style in the rest of your home. You need to consider the flow of pattern and color from room to room. If you choose a completely different style and color for each room it can be unsettling and uncomfortable to live with. Wall and flooring colors and surfaces should be as near in tone to each other as possible to make a uniform base to work from.

Dining Room

Summertime tables draw inspiration from sun-drenched gardens with shades of green and yellow mixed with a touch of blue. Table settings should not be elaborate. Use basic white china, well-made glass, and stainless steel elements for a crisp modern look. White china is a sound investment as it goes well with almost any color scheme and always makes food look appealing. Give dining room chairs a refreshing summer feel with long, pleated floral or striped slipcovers.

clockwise from top *Add a decorative touch to jars of preserves by covering the lids with fabric. Steel containers bring a contemporary feel to the table. White china looks good against distressed white or dark wood. An inexpensive way to build up a good selection of china is to keep your eyes open for discontinued lines.*

Kitchen

Diversity in shape and texture enlivens the decorating scheme of this kitchen. Yellow and green checks, trellis design wallpaper, and botanical prints are mixed with more rustic elements such as wicker and black metal. Avoid clutter by stacking stylish wicker baskets, the ideal hiding spots for your *batterie de cuisine*. Baskets are also excellent places to store fruit and vegetables—many of which have better flavor when kept at room temperature. Try the old Italian custom of lining up tomatoes on the windowsill in the sun. Apart from being decorative, there is nothing to beat the mouth-watering taste of sun-ripened tomatoes.

clockwise from top left *Keep spices organized in a distressed wooden spice rack.*
Look for interesting accessories with a botanical theme—it is a great way to add color and pattern.
Olive oils infused with herbs and spices are fantastic to cook with or as a base for delicious salad dressings.

Bedroom

With a yellow palette and splashes of white and gold, this small bedroom is turned into an elegant yet informal retreat. Sumptuous layers of bed linens and a floral-print fabric with a yellow summer rose-motif were used to create a fresh, welcoming atmosphere. White-painted distressed wooden furniture and wreath design textured wall-paper add a clean, modern touch. Look for existing pieces of furniture such as a redundant console table or chest of drawers to take on a new role as dressing table.

Bathroom

Create tactile and visual pleasure with a mix of the refined and the countrified, the traditional and the contemporary. A classic floral-print curtain and stipple stripe wallpaper are combined with the rough texture of unfinished whitewashed wood and clean-cut metal trim to create a look that is both classic and modern. Hand towels are kept neatly rolled up in a delicately hand-painted enamel bucket. Similar pieces can be found in second-hand shops. If floral-print designs are not quite up your alley, try introducing woven gingham checks or stripes.

right *Toothbrushes with clear plastic handles reflect the color theme of the bathroom.*

from left *Yellow is uplifting and warm, able to create glowing interiors. Update existing plain white bed linens with checked borders and narrow tie details. Display botanical postcards or seed packets in vertical rows with lengths of jute cording for inexpensive but fun wall hangings. Attach the cord with masking tape or glue and informally tie the loose ends at the top.*

Make a curtain with a plastic lining and contemporary tab heading for an interesting alternative to ready made shower curtains. Affix tabs with Velcro™ to make the curtain easily removable. If you have a bit of time and patience, make a fun project out of transforming existing plain enamel or steel buckets with oil paints.

e l e m e n t s

Bring a feeling of space and light to your surroundings with inspiration from the vibrant color palettes and relaxed lifestyles of far-flung, sunny places. Absorb

the intense azure of the water, the brilliance of sunlight, and the saturated greens of the landscape. Awaken your senses to the delights of free-form flowers and abstract patterns printed on voiles and cottons, spice colored canvas fabrics, loosely slipcovered furniture, and contemporary accessories. You'll create a bright look that is playful and far from ostentatious.

CREATIVE COLOR

Living Room

Give a twist to traditional floral furnishings by blending stenciled free-form patterns and bright, fresh hues. Strong colours and tactile fabric prints appeal to today's relaxed lifestyle and fit easily into the smaller spaces of modern houses. Contemporary decorating accessories with clean lines and simple shapes are best for this look. Explore ways to maximize the use of space. A good example is the rectangular woven basket with handles—a modern, portable and storable alternative to the traditional magazine rack.

clockwise from top left

Contrast intense bursts of color with brilliant white and stick to simple furnishings.

A small console table in front of a window provides space for reading and writing.

Dining Room

Combine contemporary floral prints, distressed white wooden furniture, and printed sheers for a refreshingly simple, informal, and serene dining area. Colored and clear crystal glassware adds a touch of opulence to the scheme. Look at antique shops and flea markets for glassware dating from the Thirties or browse department or chain stores for comparable styles. Sheer tablecloths are unusual, add a sense of lightness, and allow the texture of the table to shine through.

opposite *Contrast the delicate sheerness of a voile tablecloth with brightly colored plates to ensure the continuation of the decorating scheme and to add interest and detail.*

Kitchen

The homespun appearance of this kitchen is given a modern edge with the use of brilliant blues, greens, and yellows. The defined use of strong color is graphic and picks out key design elements—a bright blue cabinet and door-frame detail and rich mustard slip-covered chair—in an otherwise all-white scheme. To give this look extra zest, use highlights of contrasting color such as the luscious lime green throw. Fabric throws are effective decorating tools and are also incredibly simple to make. Instead of sliding doors and built-in units for hiding away kitchen tools, stand glass and ceramic storage jars on top of cabinets or install open shelving.

clockwise from top left *Freeform floral designs are modern yet traditional.*
Strong colors require strong flavors. For the most fragrant curry dishes, try making your own curry paste at home.
Easy-to-reach open storage is efficient and decorative and convenient for dedicated cooks.

Bedroom

The bedroom is peaceful and serene—everything is selected to hold and reflect light. The walls are covered in textured terracotta wallpaper and kept virtually bare to allow the uninterrupted flow of color. Pattern appears only as an accent in the plump comforter and cushions. The flowing lines of the large-scale floral design are echoed in the scalloped flap detail of the pillow shams. The bed is given a soft touch with a dreamy muslin canopy with inverted pleats and tie detail. A similar effect can be achieved by

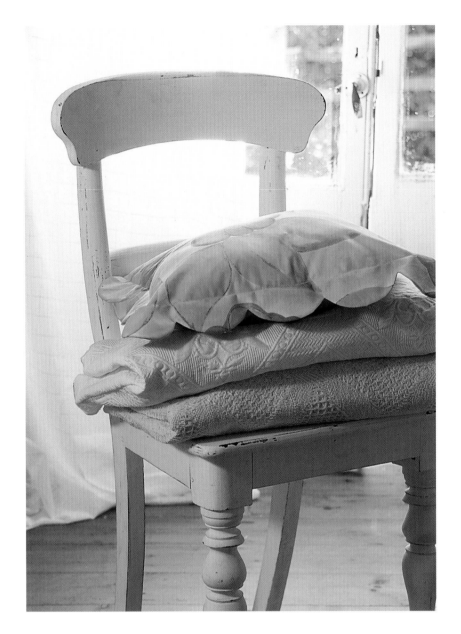

clockwise from top left *Bright colors have the most impact when contrasted with white— a combination best suited for sunny climates.*
The bright colors of nature inspired the use of color in these fabric designs.
Style does not have to be expensive. An inexpensive table wine was sold in this carafe.
Fun textured stripe and geometric wallpapers are ideally suited to this look.

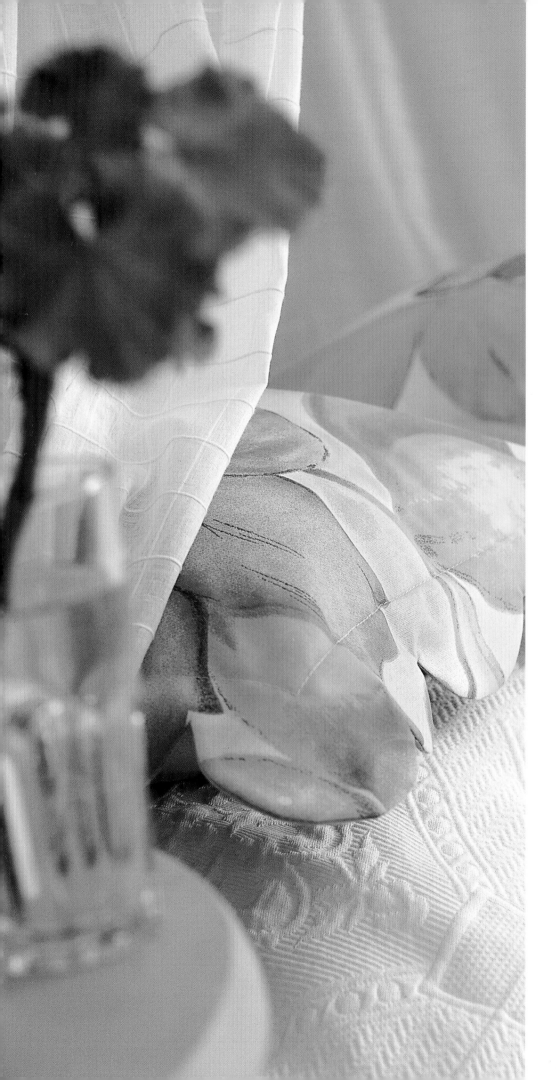

loosely draping muslin over the frame of a four poster bed. Free-standing armoires and wardrobes are stylish storage options for clothing, but perhaps not the most practical if space is limited. Nowadays, there is a much wider selection of really good-looking built-in wardrobe units to choose from. If you still can't find anything suitable, commission a reputable carpenter to custom-make a wardrobe, or consider updating an existing unit with contemporary styled doors. Sometimes a simple change—such as replacing the doorknobs—can completely alter the style. Give old trunks a new lease on life with a coat of paint or a textured paint finish. Trunks are always useful for storing smaller pieces of clothing or excess bed linens.

Bathroom

Modern shapes and utility are combined in this bathroom. A backdrop of strong color holds together a simple, understated blend of steel, wicker, and white. The hanging rail system is an innovative and contemporary storage solution—holding towels, toiletries, and even decorative accessories. Make sure there is a definite order in the way you put together displays in a system like this, and be sensitive and selective in your choice of toiletries. Look for toothbrushes with beechwood or clear plastic handles, unadorned ceramic toothbrush holders, and plain, fragrant soaps with simple, clear-cut shapes.

clockwise from top *Decant products such as day-to-day shampoos and bath oils into clear glass bottles found at most department stores or bath shops. Add a light-hearted touch with accessories such as this decorative boat.*
Look for laundry baskets with clean and simple lines to compliment this modern style.

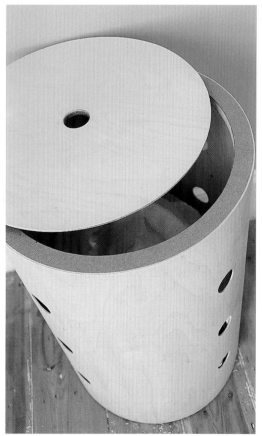

from left *Bright blues, greens, and yellows are uplifting and create a cheerful atmosphere.*

Look for fabrics with free-form floral and abstract designs and color-washed textures.

Accentuate architectural detailing with bright color for a graphic effect. You will need: White and blue emulsion paint, masking tape, brushes. Step by step: 1. Repair surface blemishes and apply two coats of white paint. 2. Mask door frame and ledges with masking tape. Rub edges of the tape carefully to secure. 3. Using a narrow brush paint between masked-off areas. Let paint dry before removing the tape.

Mix modern brights with natural elements such as light woods, and contrast with steel for a contemporary effect. Create a feeling of lightness by complementing sheers with clear crystal.

e l e m e n t s

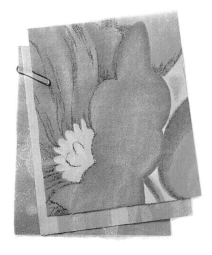

Credits

page 1 yellow glass The Plush Bazaar; tablecloth Voile Trellis Mustard Biggie Best

page 2 selection of fabrics from the Mediterranean range Biggie Best

page 3 selection of woven stripes, checks, jacquards and canvas fabrics Biggie Best

page 4 dried lemons The Bright House

page 6 curtains in Jute Muslin, pancake cushion cover in Cream Basecloth Biggie Best

page 9 deckchair cover in Provincial Biggie Best

page 10 rattan mats The Bright House

page 11 *clockwise from top left:* cushion with tie detail in Steel Blue Stripe Biggie Best; folded fabrics from the Chateaux Blue and Gold range Biggie Best; scatter cushion with rope and tassel detail Biggie Best; bed cover in Cream Basecloth Biggie Best

page 12 *top left:* Bristol chair with loose cover in Natural Canvas Biggie Best

page 13 twig urns Biggie Best

page 14 pumice Côté Bastide

page 15 *clockwise from top left:* shower curtain Victorian Bathrooms, frame City Living; cushion Biggie Best; Biggie Best chair with loose cover in Cream Basecloth and runner in Cream Basecloth and Plain Mustard Biggie Best

page 16 *top left:* tablecloth in Morocco check Biggie Best; *bottom right:* Small Sardinian Check Green Sarah Fleming

page 20 sofa in Morocco check, fabric drape in Large Navy and Fawn check, chair in Small Candy C check, sofa in foreground in Spain check and selected scatter cushions all Biggie Best

page 21 selection of scatter cushions and curtains in Biggie Best's range of woven checks.

page 23 tablecloth in Small Candy B check Biggie Best; antique plates The Plush Bazaar; terracotta pots same at The Plush Bazaar; chairs painted in Plascon Deep Forest B23-7 ; candles The Bright House

page 24 *top left:* cupboard lined with Small Sardinian Check Blue and Small Sardinian Check Yellow Sarah Fleming

page 25 *fabric from top to bottom:* Large Navy and Fawn check, Large Candy C check, Small Candy B check all Biggie Best; antique plate and fork The Plush Bazaar

page 26-27 black wrought iron bed, Terracotta Textural wallpaper, Ecru Jacquard bedspread, Multi-check patchwork quilt, Natural throw, curtain in Morocco check, Oxford pillow and scatter cushion in Small Navy and Fawn check all Biggie Best; brush and mirror set Past and Present

page 29 alarm clock The Bright House

page 30-31 toiletries Côté Bastide; Neo Classic basin and pedestal and Long Reach basin taps Victorian Bathrooms

page 32-33 *pictures from left to right:* tablecloth in Morocco Biggie Best; tablecloth in Small Candy B Biggie Best; distressed pictures Biggie Best; cushion in Spain Biggie Best; *fabric swatches:* 1. Large Navy and Fawn check and Small Navy and Fawn check 2. Spain check and Canvas Blue 3. Large Candy C check, Canvas Dark Mustard and Small Candy B check 4. Morocco and Canvas Brick 5. Green, Burgandy and Fawn check all Biggie Best

page 34 Brown Canvas Stripe and Brown Textural wallpaper Biggie Best

page 36 Brown Textural wallpaper, Buckingham Squareback sofa and Victorian Chesterfield chair both in Natural Canvas loose covers, Celton dresser, coffee table, twig urns, scatter cushions and blind in Cream Basecloth all Biggie Best; large white candle The Bright House; side table The Plush Bazaar; side table painted in Plascon Broken White G376

page 38 knitted cushion cover Biggie Best

page 39 *clockwise from top left:* Buckingham squareback sofa and scatter cushions Biggie Best; limestone bowls The Bright House; seedballs Biggie Best; candles and limestone flat dish The Bright House; Canvas Stripe Brown and Brown Textural wallpapers Biggie Best

page 40-41 tablecloth in Cream Basecloth Biggie Best; hurricane lamps and glasses Bric-a-Brac Lane; pasta bowls Continental China

page 45 cupboard painted in Plascon Frites C15-4; chair painted in Plascon Parmesan A9-2; wall painted in Plascon Paprika WAA 54; mixing bowl Bric-a-Brac Lane; hanging rail and hooks Victorian Bathrooms; throw, cupboard curtain lining in Cream Basecloth all Biggie Best

page 46-47 canopy, night frill and tablecloth in Cream Basecloth, bolsters in Natural Canvas, Textural Brown wallpaper, Ecru Jacquard bedspread, Tall Lampbase, Jacquard lampshade, Winchester chair in Jacquard loose cover, scatter cushion and White Muslin curtain all Biggie Best

page 48 *top left:* fabric drape Cream Muslin, wrought iron bed, Ecru Jacquard Bedspread and cushions Biggie Best; Sardinian Small Check Brown comforter Sarah Fleming; *bottom right:* Tall lamp base and Jute Trim lamp shade Biggie Best; frame Graphiti; *bottom left:* Bristol chair with loose cover in Natural Canvas and scatter cushions Biggie Best

page 49 bed loose cover in Cream Basecloth, Ecru Jacquard bedspread and Natural throws Biggie Best

page 50-51 curtain in Jute Muslin Biggie Best

page 52-53 throw and blind in Natural Canvas; Slipper bath, Bath Shower Mixer taps with handset, beech toothbrushes and mugs Victorian Bathrooms; waffle weave towels and soaps Bric-a-Brac Lane; toiletries Côté Bastide; basket The Plush Bazaar

page 54-55 *pictures from left to right:* Jute Muslin Biggie Best; White Muslin Biggie Best; frame Graphiti; bedcover in Cream Basecloth Biggie Best; *fabric swatches:* 1. Twill Stripe and Twill Check 2. Script Block and Script 3. Natural Canvas 4. Jute Muslin 5. Damask Natural all Biggie Best

page 58-59 blind in Olivia Tea, Celton table, button footstool in Twill Stripe Cream, Celton cupboard, Leicester sofa with loose cover in Natural Canvas and scatter cushions in Olivia Tea, Odette Tea, Rose and Dot and Olivia Pink and Blue all Biggie Best; round table Sarah Fleming; glass container Bric-a-Brac Lane

page 60 folded fabric Bramble Rose Biggie Best; old suitcase same at The Plush Bazaar

page 62 colander, canisters, enamel bucket, antique tea cups and selection of glass containers The Plush Bazaar; blind in Cream basecloth Biggie Best

page 65 tea-cosy in Ticking Pink, basket lining English Rose Biggie Best

page 66-67 cushions in Olivia Tea, Odette Tea and Odette Pink and Blue, Ecru Jacquard bedspread and blind in white muslin Biggie Best

page 68 *top right:* Celton dresser and cream photoframe Biggie Best; *bottom right:* cushions in Olivia Tea and Odette Pink and Blue; *bottom middle:* lamp base Biggie Best; *bottom left:* postcards Graphiti

page 69 Winchester chair with Olivia Tea loose cover and scatter cushions Biggie Best

page 70-71 antique bottle The Plush Bazaar; Victorian bath and Chrome Bathrack and Book Rest all Victorian Bathrooms

page 72-73 *pictures from left to right:* blind in Roses and Ribbons Biggie Best; picture The Plush Bazaar; roses Kenly Flowers; antique cup The Plush Bazaar; *fabric swatches:* 1. Bramble Rose and Ticking Pink 2. Rose and Dot 3. Natural Canvas 4. Olivia Tea and Odette Tea 5. Odette Pink and Green and Olivia Pink and Green all Biggie Best

page 76-77 curtain in Fleur de Lis white muslin and tablecloth and scatter cushion in Sardinian Wide Stripe Red Sarah Fleming; pictures on mantelpiece and table Graphiti; Winchester chair with loose cover in Twill Check Cream Biggie Best

page 80 Biggie Best chairs with loose cover in Sarah Fleming Sardinian Small

Check Red; runner in Cream Basecloth and Mini Check Red border Biggie Best; striped tins and decanter The Plush Bazaar; hanging lamp and white ceramic dish The Bright House

page 82 comforter and curtain tie-backs in Sardinian Large Check Red, lamp base, scatter cushions in Tramline Check Red and gold trim lamp base all Sarah Fleming; bed curtains in Cream Basecloth, button footstool in Twill Stripe Cream and Jute Trim Square lampshade Biggie Best

page 84 curtains in Small Sardinian Check Red and scatter cushion in Tramline Check Red Sarah Fleming; tie-on cushion in Mini Red Check and Wreath Towels Biggie Best; Cleo bath, Gold Shower Mixer, Gold Soap Dish and Gold Bathrack Victorian Bathrooms; Toiletries Côté Bastide

page 86-87 *fabric swatches:* 1. Large Sardinian Check Red Sarah Fleming, Twill Check Cream Biggie Best and Small Sardinian Check Red Sarah Fleming 2. Tramline Check Red Sarah Fleming 3. Sardinian Wide Stripe Red Sarah Fleming and Twill stripe Cream Biggie Best 4. Cream Basecloth and Mini Check Red Biggie Best 5. White Muslin Biggie Best

page 88 antique serving plate The Plush Bazaar; white emboidered napkin Biggie Best

page 90-91 Barberton daisies Kenly Flowers; curtain and scatter cushions in Floral Delight, straight-back chairs with loose covers in Damask Old Rose and Damask Gold and Winchester Chair with Damask Cream loose cover Biggie Best

page 92 curtains in Fragrant Appeal with Damask Old Rose centre borders, white embroidered napkins, Celton cupboard, Celton dining table and chairs and tablecloth in Cream Basecloth Biggie Best; flowers Kenly Flowers

page 94 *clockwise from top left:* white plate Continental China; utensils Bric-a-Brac Lane; antique china The Plush Bazaar; sieve Bric-a-Brac Lane

page 95 tablecloth in Floral Delight Biggie Best; lamp The Bright House; framed pegboard Graphiti; chairs painted in Plascon Broken White G376; walls painted in Plascon Antique White VEL6

page 96 curtains in Floral Delight and Cream Basecloth, Floral Delight comforter, frilled pillow cases in Floral Delight, Oxford flap pillow cases in Quisique and Mini Green check, set of sheets with border, Floral Delight pleated lampshades and white Candlestick lampbase all Biggie Best

page 98 curtains in Floral Delight and Cream Basecloth, scatter cushion in Fragrant Appeal and chair loose cover in Damask Old Rose Biggie Best

page 99 *clockwise from top left:* Floral Delight fabric swatch Biggie Best; Textural Green, Trellis Mustard and Textural Terracotta wallpapers Biggie Best; flowerpots Biggie Best; Emboidered Yellow and Green pillowcases Biggie Best

page 100 blind in Abingdon Rose Brick Sarah Fleming; Victorian Bath, shower curtain, Neo Classic toilet, London basin, mirror and lights, taps, toilet brush and free stading soap dish all Victorian Bathrooms; screen frame City Living; soaps Bric-a-Brac Lane; bath oil Côté Bastide

page 102-103 *fabric swatches:* 1. Abington Rose Sarah Fleming 2. Damask Cream, Damask Gold and Damask Green Biggie Best 3. Floral Delight and Cream Basecloth Biggie Best 4. Quisique and Mini Check Green Biggie Best 5. Fragrant Appeal and Damask Old Rose Biggie Best

page 106-107 curtain in Cream Basecloth with borders in Navy Dobby, Buckingham Squareback sofas with loose covers in Dobby Navy, selection of scatter cushions, rope balls, stool in Dark Mustard Canvas, Natural throw and wicker chair with cushion in Natural Canvas, Celton Dresser and coffee table, boats and lighthouses all Biggie Best; Shell pictures Graphiti

page 108 *clockwise from top left:* Geo wallpaper, Mini Check Red and Mini Check Blue fabric and Wreath wallpaper border Biggie Best; Textural Brown, Textural Terracotta, Textural Brick and Trellis Mustard wallpaper Biggie Best; Jute and Button trim cushion Biggie Best; Fish on Stick Biggie Best; Winchester chair with loose cover in small Navy and Fawn check, cushion in Canvas Brick, boats, Nautical Shadow boxes and flower pots all Biggie Best

page 110-111 map pictures Graphiti, runner in Cream Basecloth with Dark Mustard Canvas border, Biggie Best chairs with loose covers in Cream Basecloth and birds on sticks Biggie Best

page 112 tablecloth in Dobby Navy and cushion and napkins in Steel Blue Stripe Biggie Best; plates The Plush Bazaar; utensils Bric-a-Brac Lane

page 113 *middle:* drawstring bags in Steel Blue check and Dobby Navy Biggie Best

page 114 curtain in Dobby Navy and ship picture Biggie Best; striped plate The Plush Bazaar

page 115 Wedgwood plate The Plush Bazaar

page 116 selection of leather trim and chambray photoframes Biggie Best

page 117 duvet and pillowcase, Tub chair with loose cover in Steel Blue Stripe, cushions in Steel Blue Check and Steel Blue Stripe, toiletries, towel, boats and bags in Steel Blue Check all Biggie Best

page 118 blind in Dobby Navy, Canvas Natural, Canvas Brick and Canvas Dark Mustard, chickenmesh cabinet and Bristol chair with loose cover in Canvas Natural Biggie Best; limestone dish and lamp The Bright House; toiletries Côté Bastide; Victorian bath, Shower Mixer with handset and Chrome Bathrack Victorian Bathrooms

page 120-121 *pictures from left to right:* Tub chair in Steel Blue Stripe Biggie Best, postcard Graphiti; chair cover in Cream Basecloth Biggie Best; lamp and limestone dish The Bright House, toiletries Côté Bastide; boat, cushion in Steel Blue Stripe and 1"Gingham Navy and sofa in Canvas Natural Biggie Best; *fabric swatches:* 1. Geo, Mini Check Blue, Mini Check Red 2. 1"Gingham Navy, Cream Basecloth, Plain Navy 3. Canvas Natural, Dark Canvas Mustard, Canvas Brick 4. Dobby Navy 5. Steel Blue Check, Steel Blue Stripe all Biggie Best

page 124-125 curtain in Mirabelle, stool with loose cover in Canvas Blue, yellow, green and blue throws, wicker sofa with cushions in Natural Canvas, Cheltenham chair with Mirabelle Yellow loose cover, Deco lamp shade, Tall lamp base, scatter cushion in Mirabelle Yellow and Canvas Green all Biggie Best

page 127 *bottom left:* cushions in Sardinian Narrow Stripe Green, Sardinian Large Check Yellow and Canvas Mustard Sarah Fleming

page 128 *clockwise from top left:* wicker sofa, cushions in Natural Canvas, shadow pictures, topiary pots and tapestry cushion all Biggie Best; topiary pots Biggie Best; lemon pots Biggie Best; topiary pictures Biggie Best

page 129 pictures Graphiti

page 130 chair covers in Sardinian Narrow Stripe Yellow and Premula Sarah Fleming; Textural Yellow wallpaper Biggie Best

page 132 spice rack and blackboard Biggie Best

page 133 cushion in Sardinian Large Check Yellow and folded fabric Sardinian Small Check Green Sarah Fleming; Trellis Green wallpaper Biggie Best; botanical postcards Graphiti; folding chair painted in Plascon Forest B22-7

page 134-135 night frill in Mini Check Yellow, cushions in Olivia Yellow and Mini Check Yellow, pillow case with Mini Check Yellow border and ties, throw, embroidered quilt, White Jacquard bedspread Textural Wreath Yellow wallpaper and Celton furniture all Biggie Best; pictures Graphiti

page 136 curtain Flowertime, Stipple Stripe Yellow wallpaper and wooden cabinet Biggie Best; mirror City Living; glass shelves, Slipper bath, Oxford basin and pedestal and taps Victorian Bathrooms

page 137 free standing toothbrush holder and perspex toothbrushes Victorian Bathrooms

page 138-139 *fabric swatches:* 1. Mirabelle, Canvas Green and Canvas Blue 2. Leaftrail 3. Olivia Yellow and Mini Check Yellow all Biggie Best 4. Sardinian Narrow Stripe Green and Sardinian Small Check Green Sarah Fleming 5. Flowertime and Stipple Stripe Yellow Biggie Best

page 140 glass The Plush Bazaar

page 142 curtains in Floral Splash Brick/Yellow/Blue Voile, Bristol chair with Canvas Green loose cover, Cheltenham chair in Canvas Dark Mustard and canvas scatter cushions all Biggie Best

page 143 *clockwise from top left:* curtains in Floral Splash Brick/Yellow/Blue Voile Biggie Best; loose cover in Mini Check Yellow, Celton console, chair and cream photo frame Biggie Best

page 144 curtains in Floral Splash Blue on mustard, tablecloth in Voile Trellis Yellow and chair cover in Mini Check Yellow Biggie Best; blue glasses The Plush Bazaar

page 147 Cheltenham chair with loose cover in Canvas Dark Mustard and throw in Shastia Green with border in Shastia Blue Biggie Best, Wedgwood plates and mixing bowl Bric-a-Brac Lane; steel tin The Bright House

page 148-149 White Jacquard bedspread, Jacquard Oxford pillowcases, comforter and scalloped cushions in Aquarelle Floral and corona in White Muslin all Biggie Best; bird cage The Plush Bazaar

page 150 *clockwise from top left:* Celton chair, Aquarelle Floral scalloped cushion, White Jacquard bedspread and Natural throw Biggie Best; Aquarelle Stripe, Aquarelle Floral and Brittany Stripe Yellow Biggie Best; glass Bric-a-Brac Lane; selection of textured wallpapers Biggie Best; fabrics from Mediterranean range Biggie Best

page 152 cushion in Provincial Biggie Best; bath, hanging rail system, toothbrush mug and body brushes Victorian Bathrooms; bathballs, glass bottles and glycerine soaps Bric-a-Brac Lane; soap dish The Plush Bazaar

page 153 *clockwise from top left:* shell picture Biggie Best, glass bottles Bric-a-Brac Lane; yacht Biggie Best; washing bin The Bright House

page 154-155 *fabric swatches:* Voile Floral Splash Red/ Yellow/Blue and Voile Trellis Green 2. Floral Splash and Trellis Mustard 3. Aquarelle Floral, Aquarelle Stripe and Provinciale 4. Shastia Green and Shastia Blue 5. Brittany Stripe Yellow, Claudette Yellow and Claudette Blue all Biggie Best

Picture Credits

page 2 Biggie Best/photography Ryno

page 3 Biggie Best/photography Juan Espi

page 6 Biggie Best/photography Ryno/styling Tina-Marié Malherbe

page 9 Biggie Best/photography Juan Espi/styling Tina-Marié Malherbe

page 10 *bottom:* Biggie Best/photography Juan Espi/styling Nancy Richards

page 11 *middle right:* Biggie Best/photography Juan Espi/styling Tina-Marié Malherbe; *middle left:* Biggie Best/photography Juan Espi

page 16 *top left:* Biggie Best/photography Ryno/styling Tina-Marié Malherbe; *bottom left:* Biggie Best/photography Juan Espi

page 20 Biggie Best/photography Ryno/styling Tina-Marié Malherbe

page 21 *top left, top right, middle right and bottom left:* Biggie Best/photography Ryno/styling Tina-Marié Malherbe; *bottom right and middle left:* Biggie Best/photography Juan Espi

page 22 Biggie Best/photography Juan Espi

page 24 *top left:* Biggie Best/photography Juan Espi

page 32-33 *top left:* Biggie Best/photography Ryno/styling Tina-Marié Malherbe; *second from right:* Biggie Best/photography Juan Espi

page 35 Biggie Best/photography Juan Espi

page 39 *bottom right:* Biggie Best/photography Ryno/styling Tina-Marié Malherbe; *top right and middle bottom:* Biggie Best/photography Juan Espi

page 48 *middle left:* Biggie Best/photography Ryno/styling Tina-Marié Malherbe; *bottom right:* Biggie Best/photography Juan Espi

page 49 Biggie Best/photography Juan Espi

page 50-51 Biggie Best/photography Ryno/styling Tina-Marié Malherbe

page 54-55 *top left:* Biggie Best/photography Ryno/styling Tina-Marié Malherbe; *far right:* Biggie Best/photography Juan Espi

page 60 Biggie Best/photography Juan Espi/styling Tina-Marié Malherbe

page 65 Biggie Best/photography Juan Espi/styling Tina-Marié Malherbe

page 68 *bottom middle:* Biggie Best/photography Juan Espi/styling Tina-Marié Malherbe

page 72-73 *top left:* Biggie Best/photography Juan Espi/styling Tina-Marié Malherbe

page 97 Biggie Best/photography Juan Espi

page 99 *middle left:* Biggie Best/photography Juan Espi

page 117 Fairlady/photography Craig Fraser/styling Shelley Street

page 120-121 *left and second from right:* Biggie Best/photography Juan Espi/styling Tina-Marié Malherbe

page 143 *bottom right:* Biggie Best/photography Juan Espi

page 150 *top right:* Biggie Best/photography Ryno/styling Tina-Marié Malherbe; *bottom left:* Biggie Best/photography Ryno

Sources

The following suppliers offer a range of country furnishings and accessories.

U.S.

Crate & Barrel
(800) 967-6696
Pottery Barn
(800) 922-5507
Pier 1
(800) 245-4595

California

Hollyhock
214 N. Larchmont Blvd
Los Angeles, CA 90004
(323) 931-3400

Sue Fisher King
3067 Sacramento St.
San Francisco, CA 94115
(415) 922-7276

Milagros Gallery
414 First Street E.
Sonoma, CA 95476
(707) 939-0834

The Pine Mine
7974 Melrose Ave.
Los Angeles, CA 90046
(323) 653-9726

The Snow Goose
1010 Torrey Pines Rd.
La Jolla, CA 92037
(619) 454-4893

Colorado

The Artisan Center, Ltd.
2757 E. Third Ave.
Denver, CO 80206
(303) 333-1201

Southwestern by Kopriva's
2445 E. Third Ave.
Denver, CO 80206
(303) 333-2299

Connecticut

Country Folk
P.O. Box 211
Rowayton, CT 06853
(203) 655-6887

Main Street Cellar Antiques
120 Main St.
New Canaan, CT 06840
(203) 966-8348

Monique Shay Antiques
920 Main St. South
Woodbury, CT 06798
(203) 263-3186

District of Columbia

Appalachian Spring
1415 Wisconsin Ave. NW
Washington, D.C. 20007
(202) 337-5780

Park Place
2251 Wisconsin Ave. NW
Washington, D.C. 20007
(202) 342-6294

Susquehanna Antique Co.
3216 O. St. NW
Washington D.C. 20007
(202) 333-1511

Florida

When Pigs Fly
411 N. Donnelly St., #101
Mount Dora, Fl 32757
1(800) 974-4735

Georgia

The Gables Antiques
711 Miami Circle NE
Atlanta, GA 30324
(404) 231-0734

Idaho

Ann Reed Gallery
620 Sun Valley Rd.
Ketchum, ID 83340
(208) 726-3036

Illinois

Amish Folk Quilt Co.
10593 W. Touhy
Rosemont, IL 60018
(847) 827-5448

Indiana

Acorn Family Antiques
15466 Oak Rd.
Carmel, IN 46032
(317) 846-6257

Parrett/Lich Inc.
2164 Canal Lane
Georgetown, IN 47122
(812) 951-3454

Thomas H. Kramer, Inc.
805 Depot St., Commerce Pk
Columbus, IN 47201
(812) 379-4097

Kentucky

Boone's Antiques of Kentucky, Inc.
4996 Old Versailles Rd.
Lexington, KY 40510
(606) 254-5335

Maine

Handworks Gallery
Main Street
Blue Hill, ME 04614
Open summer, fall, and Christmas

R. Jorgensen Antiques
502 Post Rd.
Wells, ME 04090
(207) 646-9444

Kenneth and Ida Manko
Box 20
Moody, ME 04054
(207) 646-2595

Schueler Antiques
10 High St. (Route 1)
Camden, ME 04843
(207) 236-2770

Maryland

Stella Rubin Antiques
12300 Glen Rd.
Potomac, MD 20854
(301) 948-4187

Massachusetts

La Ruche
168 Newbury St.
Boston, MA 02116
(617) 536-6366

Leonard's Antiques, Inc.
600 Taunton Ave.
Seekonk, MA 02771
(508) 336-8585

Marcoz Antiques
177 Newbury St.
Boston, MA 02116
(617) 262-0780

Pinch Pottery/ Ferrin Gallery
179 Main St.
Northampton, MA 01060
(413) 586-4509

Michigan

Village Green Antiques
8023 Church St., Box 159
Richland, MI 49083
(616) 629-4268

Watch Hill Antiques and Interiors
330 E. Maple Rd.
Birmingham, MI 48009
(248) 644-7445

Minnesota

Christopher Blake
16296 Elm Way
Belle Plaine, MN 56011

Mississippi

Bobbie King Antiques
Woodland Hills Shopping Center
667 Duling Ave.
Jackson, MS 39216
(601) 362-9803

The Mississippi Crafts Center
Natchez Trace Pkwy, Box 69
Ridgeland, MS 39158
(601) 856-7546

Missouri

Jack Parker Antiques and Fine Arts
4652 Shaw Ave.
Saint Louis, MO 63110
(314) 773-3320

The Picket Fence
211 E. 5th St.
Fulton, MO
(573) 642-2029

Nebraska

From Nebraska Gift Shop
Historic Haymarket
140 N. 8th St.
Lincoln, NE 68508
(402) 476-2455

New Hampshire

The League Gallery
205 N. Main St.
Concord, NH 03301
(603) 224-1471

New Jersey

American By the Seashore
604 Broadway
Barnegat Light, NJ 08006
(609) 424-4781

New Mexico

Joshua Baer and Co.
116 1/2 E. Palace Ave.
Santa Fe, NM 87501
(505) 275-5630

Onorato
109 E. Palace Ave.
Santa Fe, NM 87501
(505) 983-7490

Jonathan Parks/Julie Vaughan
Antique associates of Santa Fe
839 Paseo de Peralta, Suite M
Santa Fe, NM 87501
(505) 982-1446

New York

Cobweb
116 W. Houston St.
New York, NY 10012
(212) 505-1558

C. & W. Mercantile
Main St.
Bridgehampton, NY 11932
(516) 537-7914

Country Living
26 Montauk Hwy
East Hampton, NY 11937
(516) 324-7371

Evergreen Antiques
1249 Third Ave.
New York, NY 10021
(212) 744-5664

Fisher's Main Street
Sag Harbor, NY 11963
(516) 725-0006

Gene Reed/A Country Gallery
75 S. Broadway
Nyack, NY 10960
(914) 358-3750

Gordon Foster, Ltd.
1322 Third Ave.
New York, NY 10021
(212) 744-4922

Lyme Regis, Ltd.
68 Thompson St.
New York, NY 10012
(212) 334-2110

John Keith Russell Antiques
Spring St.
South Salem, NY 10590
(914) 763-8144

Susan Parrish Antiques
390 Bleecker St.
New York, NY 10014
(212) 645-5020

Pierre Deux
870 Madison Ave.
New York, NY 10021
(212) 570-9343

Zona
97 Green St.
New York, NY 10012
(212) 925-6750

North Carolina

Cameroon's
University Mall
Chapel Hill, NC 27514
(919) 942-5554

Hillary's, Ltd.
1669 North Market Sq.
Raleigh, NC 27609
(919) 878-6633

Traditions Pottery
4443 Bolick Rd.
Lenoir, NC 28645
(828) 295-6416

Ohio

Antiques in the Bank
3500 Loraine Ave.
Cleveland, OH 44113
(216) 281-7440

Federation Antiques
2124 Madison Rd.
Cincinnati, OH 45208
(513) 321-2671

Oh Suzanna
16 S. Broadway
Lebanon, OH 45036
(513) 932-8246

Pennsylvania

M. Finkel & Daughter
936 Pine St.
Philadelphia, PA 19107
(215) 627-7797

Gargoyles Ltd.
512 S. Third St.
Philadelphia, PA 19147
(215) 629-1700

Meetinghouse Antique Shop
509 Bethlehem Pike
Fort Washington, PA 19034
(215) 646-5126

Olde Hope Antiques
Box 209, Route 202
New Hope, PA 18938
(215) 862-5055

Rhode Island

Askam and Telham, Inc.
12 Main St.
Wickford, RI 02852
(401) 295-0891

Texas

Made in France
2913 Fernadale Pl.
Houston, TX 77098
(713) 529-7949

Surroundings
1710 Sunset Blvd.
Houston, TX 77005
(713) 527-9838

Vermont

Sweet Cecily
42 Main St.
Middlebury, VT 05753
(802) 388-3353

*Vermont State Craft Center at
    Frog Hollow*
Mill St.
Middlebury, VT 05753
(802) 388-3177

Virginia

Random Harvest
810 King St.
Old Town
Alexandria, VA 22314
(703) 548-8820

Washington

Flying Shuttle
607 First Ave.
Seattle, WA 98104
(206) 343-9762

*David Reed Weatherford—
    Antiques and Interiors*
133 14th Ave. East
Seattle, WA 98112
(206) 329-6533

CANADA

British Columbia
Pathway Antiques
157 East 1st St.
North Vancouver, BC V7L 1B2
(604) 986-9282

Ontario

Art Shoppe
2131 Yonge St.
Toronto, ON M4S 2A7
(416) 487-3211

DeBoers
444 Yonge St.
Toronto, ON M5B 2H4
(416) 596-1433

UpCountry
214 King St. E.
Toronto. ON M5A 1J7
(416) 777-1700

Quebec

Décor de Campagne
1370 Zotique Giard
Chambly, PQ J3L 5T2
(888) 641-5885

INTERNATIONAL

Biggie Best International
United Kingdom Warehouse
109 South Liberty Lane
Bristol, UK
44-117-987-2722

acknowledgements

Firstly, thank you to Biggie Best International, in particular to owner Pru Pfuhl, for believing in this project and for providing unconditional support and encouragement. My thanks also to everyone at Biggie Best who have been so helpful and patient with endless requests for products and information. A huge thank you to photographer Craig Fraser for his stunning descriptive images, enthusiasm, dedication and good humour. Many thanks to Holger Schutt who energetically assisted me on numerous shoots; to Ellen Fitz-Patrick for her knowledgeable editing of my text; to old colleague and dear friend Tina-Marié Malherbe for sharing her design expertise; and to all the crafts-people involved in the soft furnishings, wallpapering and decorative painting. I must also express my gratitude to Victorian Bathrooms, Graphiti and Plascon for generously supplying products and fulfilling special requests without flinching. Thanks to my mother and father for their interest and encouragement, and above all, a big thank you to my wonderfully supportive husband Ben and our adorable baby boy, Thinus, for putting up with my too frequent absences over the past few months.